THE UNEMPTY SPACES BETWEEN

The Unempty Spaces Between
© Louis Efron / Cathexis Northwest Press

No part of this book may be reproduced without written permission of the publisher or author, except in reviews and articles.

First Printing: 2023

ISBN: 978-1-952869-78-5

Editing & Design by C. M. Tollefson
Cathexis Northwest Press

cathexisnorthwestpress.com

THE UNEMPTY SPACES BETWEEN

POEMS BY
LOUIS EFRON

Cathexis Northwest Press

A beautiful creation of song and scar, of emotional complexity and simple witness, Louis Efron's debut collection *The Unempty Spaces Between* mingles the natural and human worlds in a series of accessible, personal, universal poems. From lush to bare, the landscapes he presents us with are so intertwined with and impacted by our actions that we realize the two have always been one. Brimming with meditations deep as winter snow and boundless compassion and curiosity, these vibrant poems remain grounded in a universal familiarity that opens us up to something greater.

John Sibley Williams
author of *As One Fire Consumes Another*

Louis Efron's collection *The Unempty Spaces Between* reveals a reverence for nature and personal connection that reminds us of Mary Oliver's gorgeous nature poems. He uses language beautifully to tell us that tides "*scar* the sand," "petals color the earth/a sweet jazz composition," and "death can be a beautiful thing ... unleashing the pent-up coil spring." These poems are a deep meditation on emptiness and the searching soul.

Karol Nielsen
author of *Small Life*

The Unempty Spaces Between by Louis Efron is a refreshing work of poetry. Refreshing is the respect given to the craft of poetry. In the poetic world, where prose poetry dominates the landscape, it's refreshing to read poems marked by form and end-rhymes; notwithstanding, the journey the reader will take processing the metaphoric. Evidence of form, rhyme, and the metaphoric are signified in the poems *Lost, A Candle with Two Wicks*, and *Spaces Between*, to name a few. This work of poetry is worthy of a good read and the time of those who enjoy serious writing.

Emmett Wheatfall
author of *Our Scarlet Blue Wounds*

Haunting, harrowing and frighteningly incisive, Louis Efron's dark narrative poems incite terror, provoke gut wrenching memories and invite personal reflection. A nightmarish adventure—what could be better? *The Unempty Spaces Between* is one of my favorite afternoon reads in a decade. In his own words, "a poetic inferno," but to my mind it's "a welcome assault on the senses."

Jim Volz, Ph.D.
Editor, Shakespeare Theatre Association's *Quarto*

The Unempty Spaces Between is the product of a fellow seeker, who lives on purpose and knows that each word counts, just like each deep breath. I especially enjoyed reflecting on *God's Garden* and *Cracked* and the poetic verse of *End Game* and *Oh, Father,* to name a few. Louis Efron's poetry collection helps us to appreciate the value of living a full life, not an empty one.

Venus Jones
author of *Lyrics for Langston* and *She Rose*

What a luxury to read and soak in Louis Efron's poetry in his book *The Unempty Spaces Between*. His deeply personal poems arouse the senses with visually inducing words such as "i blew out the sun like a candle . . ." that are enhanced by their unique form to create transforming imagery and meaning. A wonderful read for introspection.

Michelle J. Kaplan
author of *and: A love story within*

The Unempty Spaces Between explores the gaps that separate us from nature, from spirit, and from each other. Louis Efron manages to fill in these "spaces between" without hyperbolic bluster or sugary metaphor. His elegiac poems take us straight to the hurt and grant a little bit of harmony to all of us "mourning our ebbing earth."

Eric D. Lehman
author of *Shadows of Paris*

The Unempty Spaces Between proves an apt title for this collection of poems by Louis Efron. These poems are tightly woven, efficient with their language, and visually make use of white space between the lines. Many of the pieces descend down the page, inviting the reader to delve deeper, by providing the room to breathe. From the first lovely poem to the last, the collection employs rich and vivid imagery, to be savored and reimagined with each reading.

Connie Soper
author of *A Story Interrupted*

For all who seek meaning in the unempty spaces between

TABLE OF CONTENTS

Beautiful Trees	17
Short Circuit	18
Home by the Sea	20
Requiem Without a Score	22
A Candle with Two Wicks	23
Empty Attics	25
Rooms Without Nightlights	27
Without Her	29
Lost	31
Little Rowboat	32
Nicked Wedding Ring	34
Oh, Father	35
Spaces Between	36
In the Eye of the Beholder	38
Requiem for a String Quartet	40
End Game	42
Arcadian Eyes	43
Writers Eulogy	45
Cracked	46
Chalk Castles	47
Reflection	49
A New Home	50
God's Garden	51

BEAUTIFUL TREES

Petrified roots cemented deep
In the rigid jaws of Earth

Arms struggling against another storm
Fruit and leaves dead yet unfallen

Thrust to crack
Crack to break

Limb to limb, serpentine rain
Fills the spaces between

Two imposing figures nestled in a wood
Crowded with figures and their long shadows

One, shades of aged grey and rippled bronze

The other, pinkish amber bleeding into raspberry veins

Both broad bodies of grit and thirst
Stamping tainted legacies into the yielding earth

Vying forever for a bit more sunlight, reaching
Down through their cracks for where shared roots

Lovingly break open the earth

SHORT CIRCUIT

like buttery oil

    briefly

spilling through streams of crystal-clear water

    energy infuses

        new life

        desperate to stay afloat

in unyielding currents

    competing for space

        in flesh

        and

            dirt

        never balanced

we flow

    bubble

        and

        separate

peering through syrupy membranes

    reaching

        for charged branches

        in stormy heavens

brilliant

    blinding

        crooked cords

allowing us to leap

    to the next seeded womb

and live again

HOME BY THE SEA

a fist full of droplets

    cast down

        from the heavens

            against glass panes

                like unsharpened diamonds

little glistening eyes

    peer out at rough surf

        nipping at the horizon

            counting everything

                they cannot save

still adjusting

    to the unfamiliar shadows

        of those we're meant to

love

    most

yet the storm advances

    and those cold tiny tears

        roll down all our smooth

surfaces

        layered over tumultuous sea

a carer's soft hands cradle

    the tender necks of children

        who may never grasp this wealth

           before them

comforted briefly

by touch

but tides that go out

    return

        disturb

           scar the sand again

    only to be captured in a moment

        washed away, but

never forgotten

REQUIEM WITHOUT A SCORE

below black umbrellas

    beating the worn shoes of

        those *grieving* on hallowed dirt

    with the rain

dyed roses wait

    to *again* be beautiful, true

        behind a stone marker

            scored just for *us*

a purpose searching endlessly

    for a title

    like a lone note longing for its

        song

in a world without *inked lines*

    our lives relinquished

        air flows freely through

        all vessels equally

        petals color the earth

    a *sweet* jazz composition

                boundaryless

a place where no keys go

    unplayed

A CANDLE WITH TWO WICKS

the floor liquefies

as they dance

    like thawing ice

        beneath blades

           of twirling figure skaters

playful reflections

    aging

        on a still pool of wax

two bodies teasing

    becoming *one*

        in a silent tango

           nearing its crescendo

    souls that cannot join further

engulfed in a briefly beautiful

    romance

        aware that it is not the first, but

           our last

                breath

                    that counts *most*

    soon to be

        lost

                                  as our surface

    again

          grows

                cold

                hardens

EMPTY ATTICS

dusty wooden planks

leading to forgotten places

    a borrowed space

        where things from the past

    wait

        to be cherished again

a mirrored music box

    tarnished gold and silver trophies

        picturesque postcards

    never sent

our *treasures*

    memories *unlit*

        by such neglected bulbs

still failing to see ourselves

    illuminated

        as dust settles *again*

        on the balconies of our mind

precious things

    boxed

        for overwhelmed hands and

            a crowded heart

bleeding batteries

                  in the back

                                  of a doll that no longer

cries

ROOMS WITHOUT NIGHTLIGHTS

Sparring with moonlight

    prying through shutter gaps

        menacing figures

        cut from a cloth

        of night's deep sky

        haunt the walls of our youngsters' rooms

        compelling little feet to rush through

        adrenaline filled corridors

            to escape

        cracked basement doors

        leaving lonely spaces

        with ruffled sheets

        to tend to their own ghosts

Now safe in the arms of loving guardians

    nestled heads

    with tousled hair

    gently sleep

    beneath stuffed beasts

But imagination tempers with age

    and villainous allies

      crawling out from

      between the covers

      of twisted fairytales

      swap darkened spaces

      for inviting masks

      fooled only by our children

            framed on forbidden trading cards

            in palmed devices

At the threshold of French-vanilla taffy wallpapered hallways

      like strained umbilical cords

      leading to once unlocked doors

            we are desperate, discarded sherpas

            in the thick of some impossible trek

            lying awake on stone-like mattresses

            grasping unread bedtime stories

            with stressed spines

            as sunlight fills our now adolescents' chambers

In rooms without nightlights

WITHOUT HER

i blew out the sun

    like a candle

smoky ghosts ascended

over a blackened backdrop

    extinguishing the brightness in my eyes

    perhaps

    forever

i didn't intend for things to go

    this far

just a light exhale

    breath caressing my lips poised toward

    the heavens

but my gut soured

my heart strained

and my lungs ever expanded

    like an overinflated balloon

    released by a child

    before a knot is briefly tied

just a sigh of momentary longing

quelled by such a soft, comforting voice

    like a feather suspended on a light breeze

but again

silence

always silence

as my palms

gripped tight to the light

callouses forming on these desperate fingers

it was too soon

for our flame to go

cold

LOST

Standing in this wide-open space
No paths to wander in sight
An empty expression on my face
No difference between day and night

No moon, stars, or sun
Nor trees or mountain ranges
No beds for water to run
A place adverse to changes

I look around, shades of dull brown
Asking how did I get here?
A nondescript, nowhere town
A rusty welcome sign says "Fear"

Do not move from where I stand
Beads of sweat, a reaching hand
Life now but a grain of sand
Seemed so important when it began

LITTLE ROWBOAT

Afloat on still, open waters

Carriage over an abyss

Sun drawing its last breath

Biting gale tunnels looming showers

A murky cotton blanket rolls across the sky

With deliberate strokes I swing the oars

Searching for shore, any shore

Another lonely night

Without lullaby

Without guiding light

Lids heavy with exhaust

Deep beneath the surface

A restless serpent awakes

Snapping of the whip

Squirming from the bowels

Of fiery molten mouth

Tarnished cold blackened rind

Adorned elongated spine

With coat of polished broken glass

Obscure sapphire marbles punched

In skull socket caverns

Piercing snout sheathing

Ribboned tongue, claw toothed

Wood creaking at the hull

Signals a menacing disturbance

My balmy palms grasp the rails

The briny foreplays teasing slaps

Arousing the buoyant vessel

A rock pillow breaks slumber of my cap

My body with no ground to anchor

Joining the sun until day breaks

My little rowboat made of sugar

Melts away in a sea of lost souls

Those who came before me shall see the light again

NICKED WEDDING RING

Big eyes, itchy fingers, inches from the plug
No rope or gun, no objection to be heard
An electric slot machine, a jackpot winning tug
A mother's wish cast aside, life was preferred

>Death brings out the very best in people
>The ugly DNA of their soul
>Self-righteousness hangs above the church steeple
>A look into a twisted peephole

The thieving sister lurking in the shadows
The lost brother brought to tears
The controlling aunt who thinks she knows
The conflicted uncle who hides upstairs

>Even before the body grows cold
>Vultures fighting over the money basket
>Papers burned to keep the stolen gold
>Jewelry hidden in the viewing casket

The hungry attorney eager to get a share
Governments caught with their hands in the pie
Creditors following the stench of dead air
There is business to be done, no time to cry

>Death can be a beautiful thing
>Allowing unspeakable evil to sing
>Unleashing the pent-up coil spring
>But who now has the wedding ring?

OH, FATHER

Adrift on lamenting clouds, an ephemeral tune
A father that no longer answers
All doors in this long hallway of doors, closed
Shadows flicker in a reflective pool of cancer

A father that cannot answer
Fingers stretch and slip, an unstoppable ascent to heaven
Shadows flicker over the skin like cancer
Eyes shut, translucent marbles in the sand

Fingers swiftly curling back, recoiling
Celluloid faces melt in the fire inside
His eyes, lost marbles in the sand
A stained vessel descends into earthly dreams

Frozen light sealed beneath undying screens
Open doors, memorials to intoxicating laughter, bittersweet tears
A bright light extinguished under a blanket of glistening mist
Floating on lamenting clouds, the briefest tune

SPACES BETWEEN

        it's not the bars but the voids between

        that imprisons our truest expression of self

the weeping trees just out of reach

sap edging beneath layered lids

syrupy glass strands briefly catching our light

distanced from the body

a burden limb

gives way by a simple

breath of wind

to the unforgiving earth below

        if dead, a crack

        alive, a bow

        separation, a honeyed lament

firm roots doggedly tunnel beneath me

hands that cradle fragile wings

a sanctuary for diverse belonging

        removed from judgment

        exposed to all

fingers poised towards ghosts, toward heaven

pushing out through unguarded gaps

flanking heat, cold shafts bend

into an elegant canopy for tears

IN THE EYE OF THE BEHOLDER

head surgically arched back, a

    drawbridge peaked

    like open arms

        adorning a pillow of silky golden

    curls

a skilled hand delicately prepares to

    carve

        a cherub's mark from a radiant

    canvas

        sharp silver puncturing milky

    skin

        a tear of blood rolls up a stained

    cheek

        filling an obscure oval ruby pool

a willing sacrifice

    under stark white lights

an inspired surgeon

    creating a signature work called

        PERFECTION

a gasp for air

a heartbeat

        ceases

  a blemish *too deeply* rooted in the

          soul

                removed

       an exchange for life

a bladed artist's

       muse

           so near *perfection*

               cast

                   aside

                      DEAD

    in a heavenly body of

perfect beauty

REQUIEM FOR A STRING QUARTET

wood arms bud

        stretch sunward

    and

softly sway

        deeply veined ruby-bronzed

leaves conduct

        visceral vibrations

                in melodious winds

like warm knives dividing blocks of stiff maple butter

        hungry chainsaw blades

in calloused hands

                slide through trunks, weakened

like old, hinged attic doors creaking downward

        woodland torsos slam shut against taut soil

        leaving fleeting impressions

                at the base of forgotten podiums

once pretty

        unkempt bark faces

        now polished

faceless

    beneath strings

        of weeping instruments

            orchestrated to lull those

mourning our ebbing earth

END GAME

Earthy, resilient, harshly frail
Fingertips sliding, glass shards on braille

Dirty hands mar clean frosty cloth
Moving fast, then a deadening sloth

Frozen grins thawing to disturbing frowns
Inspiration fades, struggles, and drowns

Purpose, labor, an enduring cause
Crushed to death in powerful jaws

Love, a sweetly sung lullaby
Muted by painful excuses to cry

God, existence, meaningful living
A darker force, anxiety, misgiving

Expression in art, music embraced, delight
A deafening death march, an unwilling plight

ARCADIAN EYES

dark eyes reflect smokey flashes

    from deafening staccato machine guns

        fixed on three-dimensional flat screens

fingers scurry over wireless consoles

    like spider legs attempting to evade death

        from hunched lumbering gamers

a binary coded world

    never burning

        but always on fire

            forcing sweat to boil from our pores

            to cool tranced, agitated monsters

thick layers of masked decay

    melt from our lit faces

        like wax partitions between

            real, fake

            human

            artificial

in this crowded metaverse

    where all has been equaled

and corrected

we are lonely

a world that can no longer be unplugged

where soft hands without heartbeats join

then pass through

to emptiness

WRITERS EULOGY

another day breaks through spent hourglasses

    on painted wooden windowsills

        warming settling sand

            as writers labor to create anew

rooms measure time in syllables

    emotions pool around us in ink

        white space ignites blue then orange

            a poetic inferno departing in drifting ash

blistering paper slowly curls from aging walls

    giving new breath to hidden veneers

        dusty tales sealed in glue, crack

            like thick makeup on an old face

faux leather chairs, grand desks of pine

    overlaid with shallow oak

        tarnished gold-plated trinkets adorn corniced shelves

            with forgotten fiction and others' truths

a space where everything is briefly real

    and past narratives

        bookmark time

            in bright, but empty rooms

CRACKED

If I took a hatchet to my skull
The matter would be pinkish, white
A cotton candied paintbrush swirling
Chemical hues on spongy palettes

The matter is not black or white or grey
Cellophane messengers meandering in, out of folds
Stirring chemicals spreading darkened tones
Broken junctions too wide for thoughts to leap

Tired souls recoating vibrant pigments growing dull
Peering out a broken window to gleam purpose
Delivering energy to desperate thoughts, empty canvases
Severed pathways, a million puzzles forced into disarray

Focus fades into a shadowy mosaic of abandoned dreams
Dissipating chemicals, churning into spent trays of hope
Crooked corridors lead to more and more dead ends
If I finally take a hatchet to my skull

CHALK CASTLES

Smoky ghosts writhe from the barrels of silver guns

small bodies fall upon asphalt puzzles

    settling beneath

two-dimensional makeshift playgrounds

    framed with rainbow chalk castles

branchless trees

    in the shadows of majestic turrets

and crooked hopscotch squares

crimson streams flow through our mother's taut fingers

    into tiny ravines

        from the punctured hearts of angels

empty shells hit the ground

    like tattered shoes tapping empty spaces

    between lines on sunbaked tarmac

An absent god wakes

    in a frameless sandbox of souls

blueberry powder skies morph monochrome grey

swirling winds swiftly carry away multicolored dust

    fervently feeding on a fallen paradise of little excess

      wide eyed pools peer heavenward

            pleading through narrow barred windows

   as our castles crumble inwards

         washed away by an overflow of tears

               to make way for tomorrow's

unanswered prayers

REFLECTION

Again, pulling myself out of bed
Stumbling to a bathroom mirror
Its cold surface reflects a face of dread
Could life at this moment be any clearer?

       Loved ones passed, conversations lost
       Closed doors, sunlight eludes the day
       Grass covered with frost
       Sky a disturbing grey

Not a soul in distant sight
No human touch to be had
A self-inflicted human plight
Red plumes on white, a lethal cleansing pad

       Open spaces, less machine exhaust
       Down an empty street I stray
       A non-discriminate holocaust
       Children can no longer play

What has happened to our life?
Where did it all go wrong?
Recklessly wielding a butcher knife
Lamenting lyrics . . . a troubling song

       A rhyme that riffs a careless scrawl
       A world in desperate need of peace
       Two hands dropping a wanting ball
       A time that now must cease

What will tomorrow's reflection hold?
Blood-stained cheeks, sockets conspiring to swell
Clocks stop ticking before the story is told
Doors now open, a quick descent to Hell

A NEW HOME

Unbreathable air, spoiled soil, cancerous streams
A death march of lambs to yet another slaughter

Carelessness, disease, hate, and violence
Bodies in the streets, crimson rose stained pavement

Turning away from indiscretions, mistakes
A merry-go-round of toxic horses, civil unrest

The simplest empathy like misplaced keys
A home with locked doors, window slivers void of light

A white robed preacher, a sold-out sermon with a pulpit queue
Flailing and accusatory hands, dark eyes piercing pews of repentant souls

A failed Earth, a time to discard
Another world, our new home

Your golden lottery ticket to escape the raped and pillaged
A stem pushing through the dirt to prove its worth

GOD'S GARDEN

where her tears slip and settle
    wide-opened daisies are born

shades of powdery pink and white
    bowed angelic fingers
        lifting up beaded golden saucers

light breezes sweep weeping petals
    broken pinwheels
        seed imperfect copies
as tears wilt with everything

soft wings brittle
    scatter like dandelions
        across unsettled fields
            in heavy gales

discarded vessels droop
    brown
        and
            barren
a wasteland wholly stripped of faith

a grief deeply
    dampens her earth
inspiring all that may one day

            again be beautiful

Acknowledgments :

Academy of the Heart and Mind: End Game, Little Rowboat, and Spaces Between

Literary Yard: Lost and Nicked Wedding Ring

New Reader Magazine: In the Eye of the Beholder, Beautiful Trees, Oh, Father, and Cracked

POETiCA REViEW: A New Home

A special thank you to my wife, Evie, my first and most important critic, my daughters, Anya and Ella, the best gifts my wife ever gave me, my dear parents and grandparents in heaven, my agent, mentor, and friend, John Sibley Williams, my dedicated and collaborative publisher, C. M. Tollefson at Cathexis Northwest Press, the beautiful and talented poets, authors, and artists who endorsed my book, John Sibley Williams, Karol Nielsen, Emmett Wheatfall, Jim Volz, Ph.D., Venus Jones, Michelle Kaplan, and Eric D. Lehman, and Connie Soper, the previous publishers of some of the poems included in this book, *Academy of the Heart and Mind, Literary Yard, New Reader Magazine,* and *POETiCA REViEW,* and all my readers, supporters, family and friends.

Louis Efron is a writer and poet who has been featured in *Forbes, Huffington Post, Chicago Tribune, POETiCA REViEW, The Orchards Poetry Journal, Academy of the Heart and Mind, Literary Yard, New Reader Magazine* and over 100 other national and global publications. He is also the author of four other books, including *How to Find a Job, Career and Life You Love; Purpose Meets Execution; Beyond the Ink*; as well as the children's book *What Kind of Bee Can I Be?*

Louis has worked and lived across the US, Europe, Africa, and Asia. In addition to his career as a writer, he has worked on Broadway, as a senior leader in top Fortune 500 companies, and is an expert in leadership and organizational culture. He holds an undergraduate degree in theatre arts and advanced degrees in law and psychology. He is also the founder of The Voice of Purpose and the charity World Child Cancer USA. He can be reached at LouisEfron.com.

Also Available from Cathexis Northwest Press:

Something To Cry About
by Robert Krantz

Suburban Hermeneutics
by Ian Cappelli

God's Love Is Very Busy
by David Seung

that one time we were almost people
by Christian Czaniecki

Fever Dream/Take Heart
by Valyntina Grenier

The Book of Night & Waking
by Clif Mason

Dead Birds of New Zealand
by Christian Czaniecki

The Weathering of Igneous Rockforms in High-Altitude Riparian Environments
by John Belk

If A Fish
by George Burns

How to Draw a Blank
by Collin Van Son

En Route
by Jesse Wolfe

sky bright psalms
by Temple Cone

Moonbird
by Henry G. Stanton

southern athiest. oh, honey
by d. e. fulford

Bruises, Birthmarks & Other Calamities
by Nadine Klassen

Wanted: Comedy, Addicts
by AR Dugan

They Curve Like Snakes
by David Alexander McFarland

the catalog of daily fears
by Beth Dufford

Shops Close Too Early
by Josh Feit

Vanity Unfair and Other Poems
by Robert Eugene Rubino

Destructive Heresies
by Milo E. Gorgevska

Bodies of Separation
by Chim Sher Ting

The Night with James Dean and Other Prose Poems
by Allison A. deFreese

About Time
by Julie Benesh

Quomodo probatur in conflatorio
by Nick Roberts

Suspended
by Ellen White Rook

Coming To Terms
by Peter Sagnella

Call Me Not Ishmael but the Sea
by J. Martin Daughtry

Cathexis Northwest Press

www.ingramcontent.com/pod-product-compliance
Lightning Source LLC
Chambersburg PA
CBHW030139100526
44592CB00011B/958